Give It To God And Know Peace

Journal

HOPE WINTERS

This Journal

Belongs to

____

Dear God,

I am giving this concern to you.

I know you will resolve this in the

best possible way for all concerned

Amen

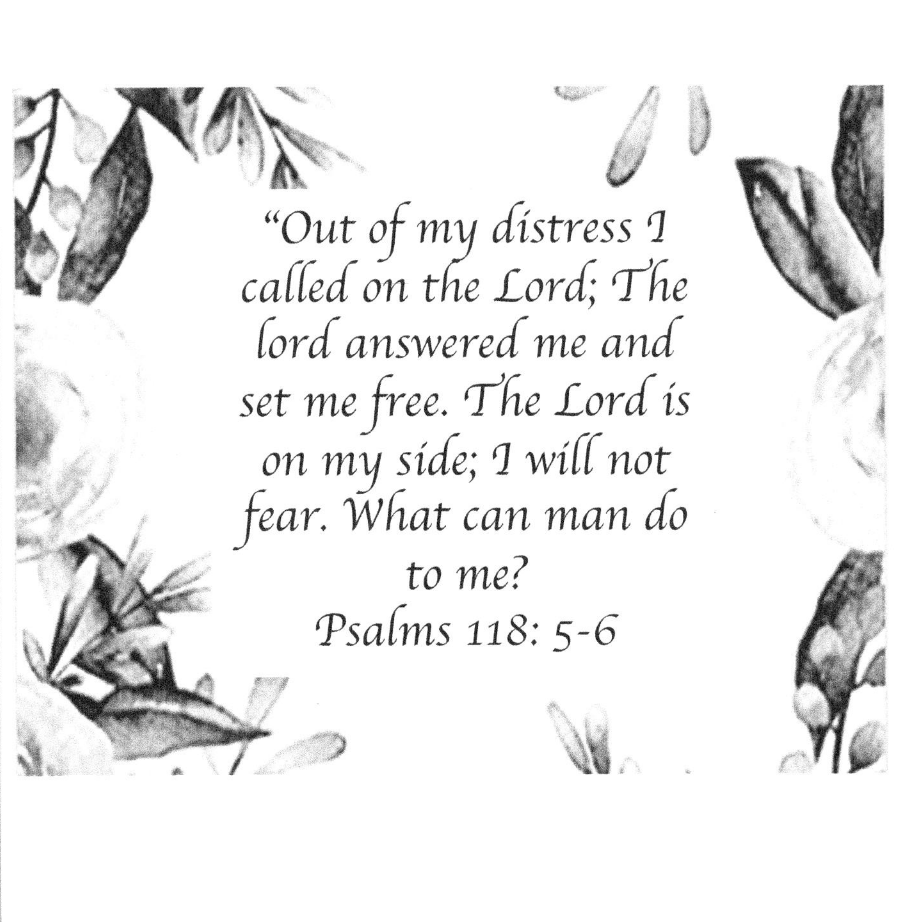
"Out of my distress I
called on the Lord; The
lord answered me and
set me free. The Lord is
on my side; I will not
fear. What can man do
to me?
Psalms 118: 5-6

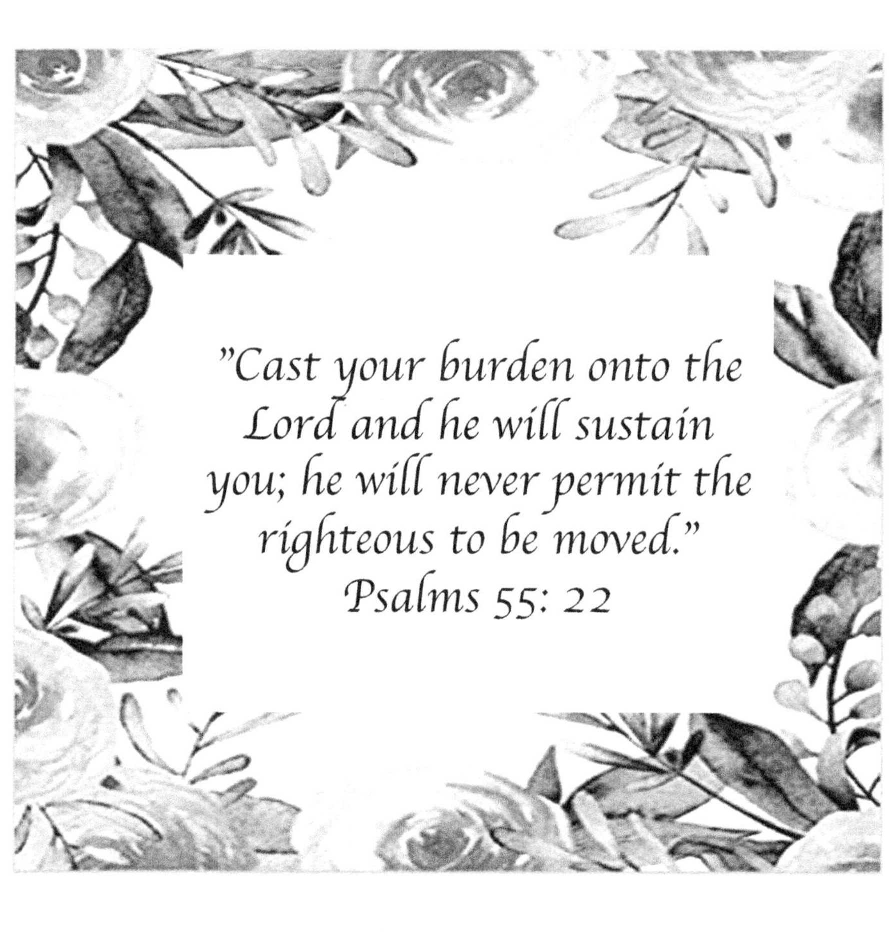

"Cast your burden onto the Lord and he will sustain you; he will never permit the righteous to be moved."
Psalms 55: 22

"For I know the plans I have for you, declares the Lord, plans for welfare and not evil, to give you a future and a hope."
Jeremiah 29; 11

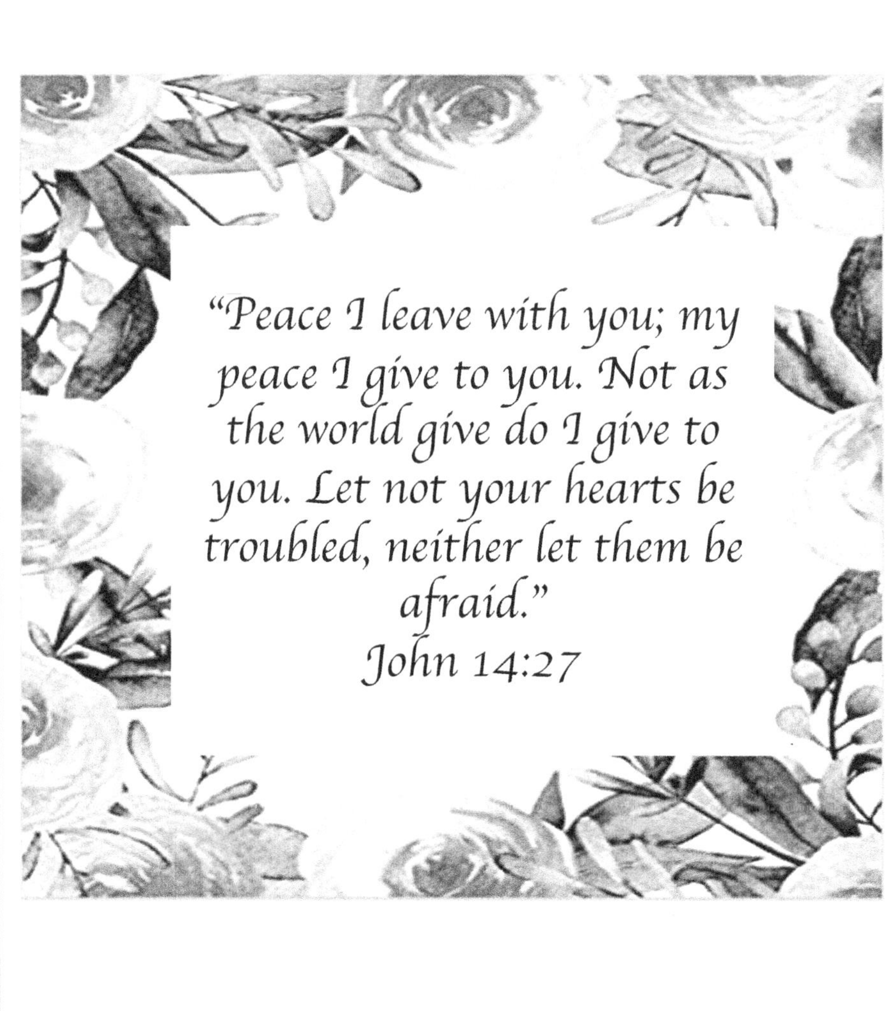

"Peace I leave with you; my peace I give to you. Not as the world give do I give to you. Let not your hearts be troubled, neither let them be afraid."
John 14:27

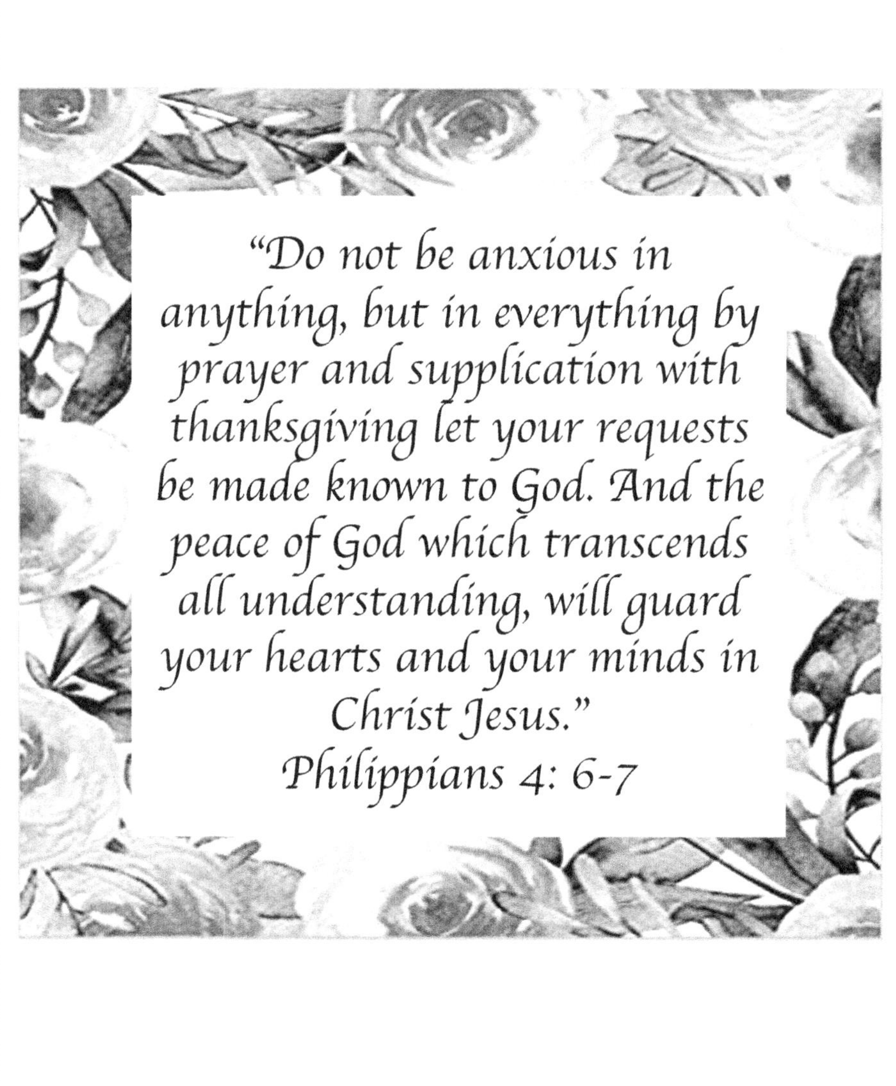

"Do not be anxious in anything, but in everything by prayer and supplication with thanksgiving let your requests be made known to God. And the peace of God which transcends all understanding, will guard your hearts and your minds in Christ Jesus."
Philippians 4: 6-7

"Fear not, for I am with you; be not dismayed, for I am your God; I will strengthen you, I will help you, I will uphold you with my righteous right hand."
Isaiah 41: 10

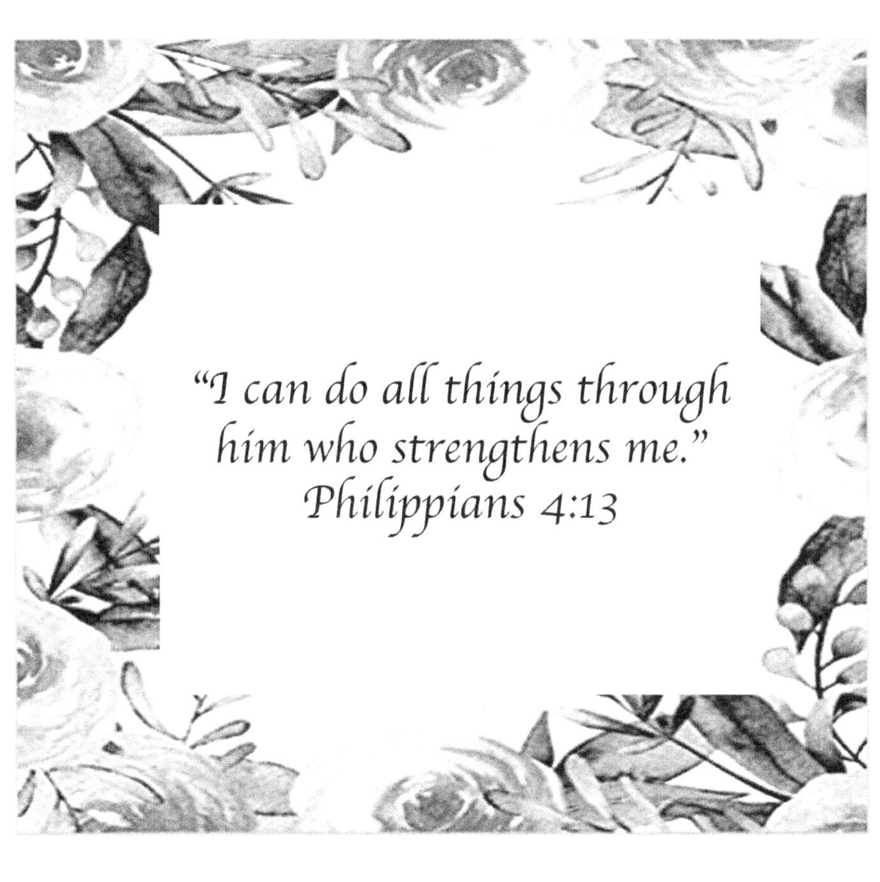

"I can do all things through him who strengthens me."
Philippians 4:13

"Anxiety in a mans heart
weighs him down, but a good
word makes him glad."
Proverbs 12: 25

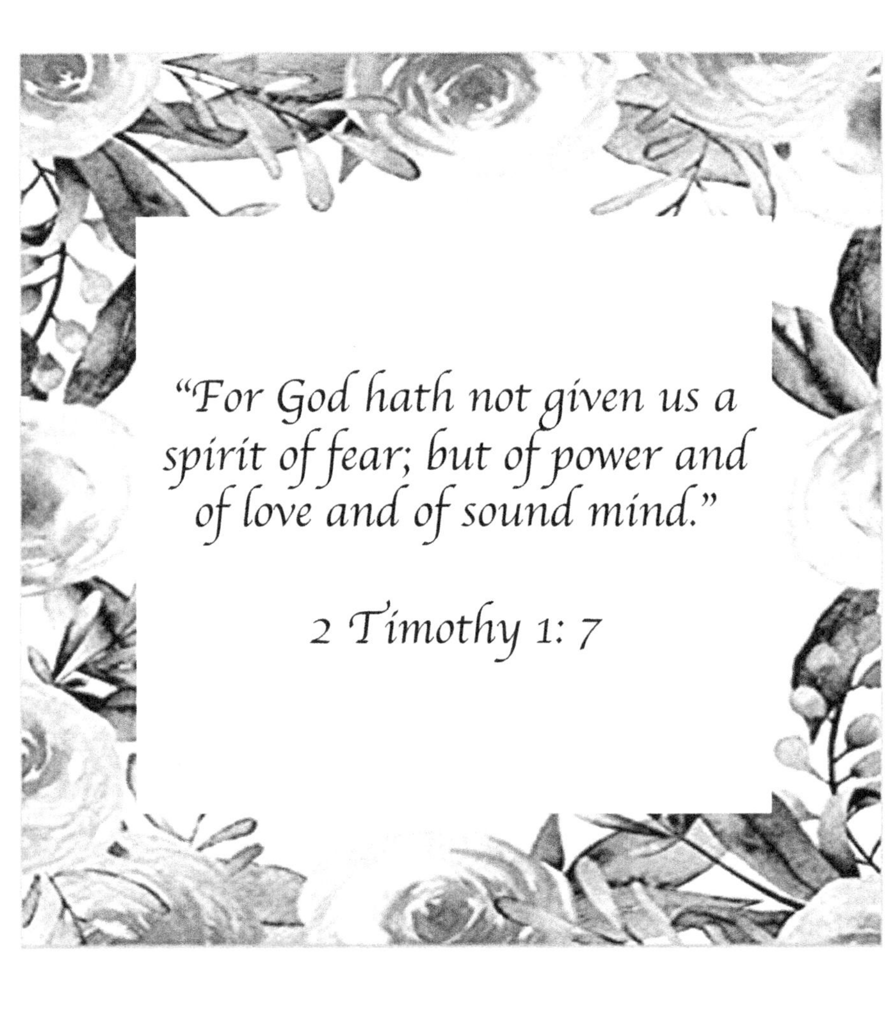

"For God hath not given us a
spirit of fear; but of power and
of love and of sound mind."

2 Timothy 1: 7

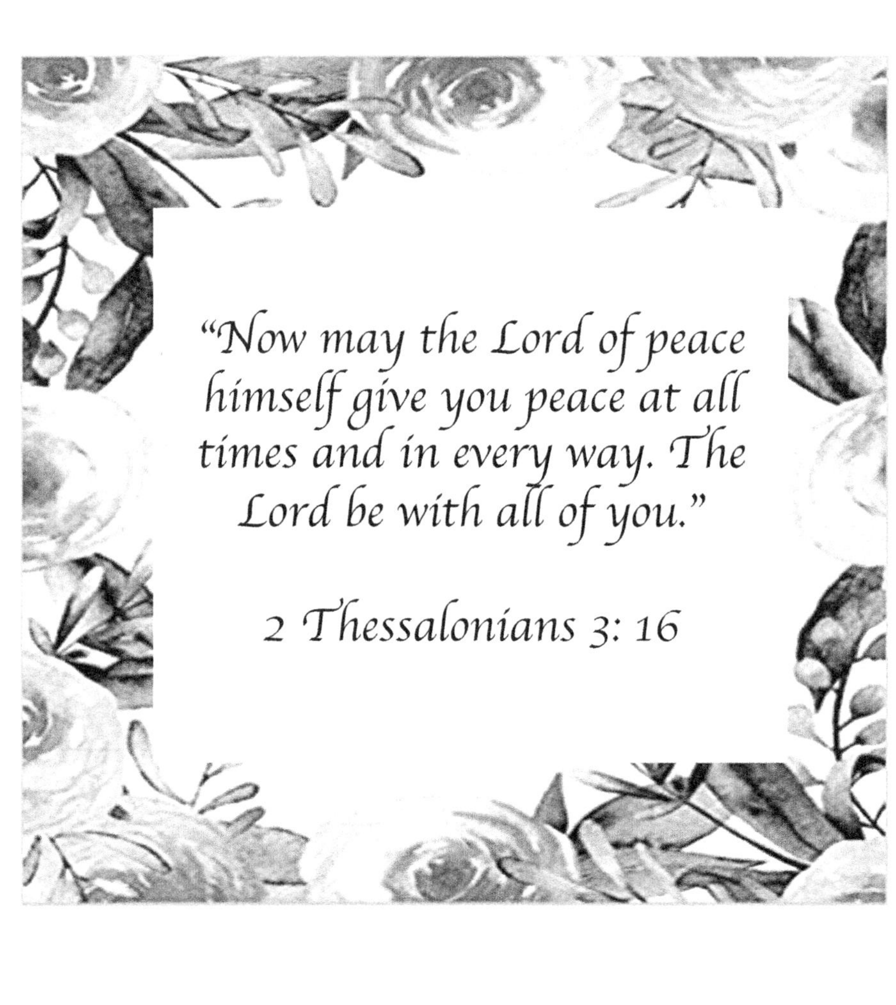

"Now may the Lord of peace himself give you peace at all times and in every way. The Lord be with all of you."

2 Thessalonians 3: 16

Made in the USA
Monee, IL
07 July 2026

56544289R00066